A LETTER TO MY LATE MOM

A LETTER TO MY LATE MOM

Copyright © 2020 Victor Ansor. All Rights Reserved.

No rights claimed for public domain material, all rights reserved. No parts of this publication may be reproduced, stored in any retrieval system, or transmitted in any form or by any means, electronic, mechanical, recording, or otherwise, without the prior written permission of the author. Violations may be subject to civil or criminal penalties.

Library of Congress Control Number:

ISBN: 978-1-7349631-2-0 (hardback)
ISBN: 978-1-7349631-0-6 (paperback)
ISBN: 978-1-7349631-1-3 (eBook)

Cover Design by Victor Ansor

VICTOR ANSOR PUBLISHING

310 Fulton Avenue Hempstead
NY 11550

Email: victoransorpublishing@yahoo.com

Printed in the United States of America

A Letter to My Late Mom

A Boy's Poetic Discourse with His Late Mother

VICTOR ANSOR

VICTOR ANSOR
PUBLISHING

There is nothing like the love of a mother for her son, nothing- I mean nothing.

Mothers are Angels, they will always be.

Also, by Victor Ansor

The Spirit of Servanthood

How to Be Ten Times Better than Your Peers

War in The Heavens

Global Holocaust

CONTENTS

Dedication 9

Prologue 10

A Letter to My Late Mom 12

Fatherless 162

Pen of A Ready Writer 165

My Lady 167

Wild and Free 168

katko vs Briney 169

The Sinner 171

Dedication

To those raised by a single mom, this is for you.
To those loved by a mother, this is for you.
To those raised without a mother, this book is for you.

May the light continue to shine on your path, and may you ride on the wings of angels gliding to a future most glorious.

Prologue

Mama, it has taken me twelve years to write this letter to you. It was not easy penning down every word because it makes more meaning to me than anyone could imagine. I still cannot bring myself to the reality that you are no more. I keep updating this letter till now that I decided to send it to you. Please while reading this letter in the privacy of your heavenly bliss, remember that your baby boy has gone through a lot emotionally, psychologically, and physically in writing this first piece.

The love that I have for you mama, is the love that a true son has for a true mother who was selfless and good beyond fault. I may not speak the mind of everyone in the family, but I do believe that the rest of the siblings have an undying love for you. We miss you mama, we do. Please remember us in your prayers and continue to watch over us, now that you have a better view of life. I hope to hear from you in your reply. Much love.

A Letter to My Late Mom

Mama, I wish I could turn back the hands of time
To the days when you were here
Remembering you every day
Tears flow down my heart silently

I wish you were still here
I cannot undo what nature has done
It is the way of all the earth
Some early some later
But all mortal must answer that call

I have come to believe a saying
That good people die young
But only when they are
Through fulfilling a purpose
So, all I can do is but wish

I never open my eyes to see my father
Yet you were more than a father to me
And all that a mother could be

You raised seven of us without a dime
Help or support from nowhere
And here I am a man that you had hoped
My heart yearns for you at
This very moment, mama
I grief and refuse to be comforted
Because I have lost a part of me to eternity

Mama, I love you and will always do
I hope you while resting are by my side

Since you left
Life has not been easy
I suffered more than I could imagine
Without help from anywhere
If not for God, the unseen father
I don't know what would
Have happened to me
The scripture says
"If your father and mother forsake you
I the Lord will take you up"
He certainly took us up
That is why we have not joined you yet

Mama in your absence
I have been through a lot
Your baby boy had to face life alone
No friends or family members to talk to

A Letter To My Late Mom

I make decisions all by myself
Some disastrous some good
I made costly mistakes
And paid the price
Bearing the consequences all but alone

I have been beaten battered
And even homeless
Maybe if you were around
Your prayers
And words of comfort would
Have soothed the moment
Challenges manifest every day
Without anyone to confide
I keep to myself

I wonder how proud I will be
On the day of my wedding
Will I rejoice because I have found a wife
Or will I mourn because I lost a mother
Who will advise me when I go wrong?
How will I tell my children
I do not have a mother
Or when they request to see their grandma
Will my wife have advice and care?
From me as she in need of a mother-in-law?
Who will come for uman-eyen?
Or bath the baby on the laps

Victor Ansor

Whom did you leave to
Carry your grandchildren?
Or tell my wife she is wrong when she errs
Or call me to question
When I stray from the path
These questions I need answers
Answers that must come
To wipe away all my tears

I only walk with my shoulders high
Pretending all is well
But burdened with the grief of loss
With nothing to hold onto in life
Except 'hope' that one day
I will see you again
But not soon mama
Not soon

If all of life pleasures are taken from me
But you were spared to be with us
Mama, no greater loss can be experienced
That you are no more
It pains me to my bone marrow
I still cannot comprehend why
It is a reality that refuses to be real to me
I wonder when I will get over it
Surely, I will never get over it

A Letter To My Late Mom

Mama, the family is torn apart
With lack and confusion
The 'lack' is love, not money
I wish the reverse were the case
And love found its proper place among us
You were the only source of unity
A mother you truly were
Please look down from heaven and help
Your love for us was truly our covering

Mama, I am now a fully-grown man
A man indeed and not yet married
I know you will scream 'why'
But be patient I will tell you why

My pageant you supported
Recorded seven editions
My company has enlarged with more ideas
Ideas that are still on paper
And yet to come alive

I have more and bigger dreams
Dreams of great things
And high places
Therefore, I continue to knock
Knock on heaven's door
For it to be open for me
That my fame and fortune can manifest

Victor Ansor

I have a lot to tell you about myself
But first, let me share with you
What has been happening in the family
I will start with the eldest, Mma your first

Mma had a fiancé before you left
His name is Rocky if you will recall
Despite his nasty attitude
He did something that you
Must thank him for
He carried you from the hospital
Back home after you died
He was helpful during
Your burial with his car
Please thank him
Whenever you are disposed

Let me whisper to you something
That will shock you
Mma was pregnant during your burial
So, if you had stayed a bit longer
You will have carried your first
Grandchild in your arms
Now they have a son
A boy whom I believe will
Soon break many hearts

A Letter To My Late Mom

After their first son, Mma and
Rocky decided to get married
During the whole wedding process
I was kept in the dark
Finally, Mma told me that I cannot
Sit as a father at her wedding
When I asked why because I was surprised
She said am not the same father with her
I was disappointed
So disappointed I refused to attend

Mma did the unspeakable and denied me
She denied my right as the first male
She embraced family members
Whom I have never seen
And made them chief at her wedding
She told me I cannot collect her bride price
Because we are not from the same father
I was heartbroken because of those words
Other siblings felt bad as well
Some refused to attend because of that

We grew up together under your care
A father we never saw
Mma is my sister and me her brother
Why should a wedding bring distinction?
A distinction that was never thought about

Victor Ansor

I remember when we use to share things
We ate from the same plate
Laugh together and cried together
When we saw other children with their father
We envied them together
And wish ours was with us
We did not see ourselves
As from different fathers
But time made a wedding to define us
My senior sister, I love so much
Told me to my face am not from
The same father with her

For this reason, I refused to attend
It was good I did not
Than to go and sit a stranger
Family members called and asked why
But I refuse to tell the reason until now
I have forgiven her and hold no grudge
But nothing can undo the thought
Of missing my sister's wedding

Mama if you were here
This will never happen
The thought of it gives me misty eyes
The scripture says *"a child shall die at a hundred,*
There shall not be an old man
Who has not fulfilled his days."

A Letter To My Late Mom

Your passing proof contrary
Because you were cut off in your prime
September was your birthday
And will always be
We would have celebrated your sixty-one years
But now that you are no more
Things are not the same
I know you will not be happy with Mma
When you read this
But loving and compassionate
You were here on earth
I know you will smile and correct her
With a gentle scourge of a mother

Mma is now a mature, responsible woman
With a family of her own to look after
Like you, she is strong and determined
She now drives her car
Given to her by her husband
She is dark, average height
Not skinny and not fat
With a strong but beautiful face
It tells on her she is stressed
But still carries herself with confident
Saying 'I can handle it'
Mma still works in that establishment
Can you please ask her to leave?
Before it is too late
It bothers me a lot

Mama do not expect me to
Talk about myself
I have so much to say
So, I keep it until the end.

Nne-ete is next in this discussion
A married woman now
With a family of her own
She is still light in complexion
The only one to take after you
The same height you left her with
And very much of a strong character
She has amazed the whole family
And a wonder to many
She is now a certified medical doctor
A dream you had years ago
Who would have believed years past?
That you will have a
Medical doctor as a daughter
She is the pride of the family I must say
A qualified doctor indeed

But after your burial
She had some issues in medical school
And was behind in some courses
Then asked to repeat a year
The rumor went around the family

A Letter To My Late Mom

That she has been expelled
Nobody believed she was
Still in medical school
She was a constant point of ridicule
Hurt and disturbed she lost weight
So skinny they thought she had a disease
But the enemies were put to
Shame when she graduated
With that joy, Nne-ete became fat overnight
Now she works in a government hospital
Attending to the needs of people

I remember how you first sowed
The seed of social service
When you cooked for
Patients in the hospital
Both psychiatric and
Teaching hospitals in Calabar
Now God has repaid you with a
Child to do it professionally

Yet I must say this mama
There is something you
Must talk to Nne-ete about
She is very bitter with Kokoete
So bitter she does not talk to him anymore
I have tried to bring peace
But she is very adamant

A mother with a soothing tongue
Will do the magic
Please step in and bring peace again

Koko your namesake is back from oversea
She was sick with news of your demise
Something she will not
Recover in a long while
Still skinny but very busty and tone
When I told her you were gone
She collapsed and was hospitalized
By divine providence
She regained consciousness
But not without a tear for you in a day
She is now managing her farm business
With a grant from the federal government
Not remarkably successful because
She was deceived and sold a swamp
For a land, now the business
Has no future due to flood
A strong woman she has become
Although yet to be married

Koko is a virtues woman I must say
Am so proud of her as my sister
She took after you in all things
With a caring and loving heart
I am owing her some money

A Letter To My Late Mom

Yet she never asked
Very patient and understanding
A virtue only you had
Considering how much I owe you myself
I pray for her every day
That a good man will come her way soon
For I know if you were still here
You would have prayed
Her into marriage by now

Love is as strong as death
I love you, mama, I must say
At this moment I cannot help but cry
As I remember everything about you
It takes great pain to write this letter
Every word makes meaning to me
If by chance this gets into another hand
I don't believe they will
Understand the content

There is nothing like the love of a mother
A selfless and sacrificial mother you were
Many mothers have done virtuously
But you excel above them all
You always give me to eat
While you go hungry
You took me shopping
For things I needed

Victor Ansor

Things I will not think
Of getting for myself
You advised me and
Taught me things
Things only a father
Could have taught his son

You showed me the way of life
How to think like a man
And act in public
To compose and carry
Myself with dignity
To dress well and be neat
Even with one cloth
To treat people well
And look out for others
To love and care for my family
And be patient with people
To respect the elders and
Authorities, and be law-abiding
To pay my tithe
And sit still in church
Till service is over
To read my bible always and pray
When I wake up in the morning

You told me, not to give
Myself to drinking alcohol

A Letter To My Late Mom

And to avoid beer parlor
To stop smoking
And be mindful of girls
To not go around breaking their heart
To reserve my strength
For the right one in the future
For they flocked around me always
Simply because of my beauty
This I failed woefully mama

Mama, you said I should
Be quick to hear and slow to speak
To have confidence in myself
While trusting in God

You took me to church
And pointed me to Jesus
The best gift you ever gave to me
For when the world failed, and friends left
The Jesus you introduced me to stays on
He's been with me mama
A friend better than any in the world
He sticks and refuses to give up on me
Guiding me all the way
To eternal rest, I believe

I remember how you held my hand
And blessed me one day

Victor Ansor

You said to me, papa
God will always bless you
Above your equals
You will become very great in life
And be a blessing to the world
You said to me that the world
Will soon celebrate me
You blessed me because
I returned from school and decided
To go and sell cold water
And use the money to buy food
For the entire family
I was fourteen years old

Oh mama
Where are you?
I am forced to face life without you
All that I live by now
Is what you taught me
If I say I don't miss you
Then I am the worst liar
I believe you are in a better place
But no better place will you be
Than with all your children
And grandchildren

I am lonely I must tell you
I do not have anyone to talk to

A Letter To My Late Mom

No one seems to understand me as you did
I have been grossly misunderstood
Ignored, betrayed, despised, and hated
I am in this world as nobody
I wish you were here mama
I cannot help but cry

Let me wipe my tears and continue
For I moist the paper with my tears
Blinded by the drops of water from my eyes
The same water that flowed like a river
On the night of your vigil
The same that flowed at your grave
Watching you with pain as you descend
Lowered into the earth
I lost control and wept
Wept bitterly as I have never wept before
Refusing to believe that it was you

I told my pastor that I love you
Love you so much that I do not think
I will love my wife the way I love you
He looked at me curiously
With a spiritual accent, he asked
Did you take an oath together?
Twisted in his thought about
The kind of love I meant
Do not blame him, he never wore my shoes

Else he would have understood
The love of a son for his mother
A love beyond any definition of love
The love that makes a man hurt
Anyone who disrespects his mother
The love that makes a son
Cherish his mother above all
Such love is difficult to destroy
It is far beyond the love of a man for a woman
It transcends time and speaks volume
That is what that pastor did not understand

Don't be displeased with this pastor, mama
For I had a bad dream one night
A scary one
Where I saw you as I usually do
For you showed up always in my dreams
And this night I called the pastor
And he prayed for me
He declared an end to you
Showing up always in my dreams
Mama since that prayer
I never saw you again
I know that was not you
Because you cannot be in heaven
And still disturb me in my dreams
Please don't forget to thank the pastor
For that great deliverance

A Letter To My Late Mom

Mama, we used to believe you
Will be old and gray
Visiting the house of
Your children in turn
We used to joke about
Whom you will stay with
Each saying they will want
You to stay in their house
If this is a dream, then I must wake
Wake to your loving smile
And comforting words
Wake and refuse to sleep
For fear of having such a dream again

Obong your son
Is a grown man now
With two university degree
I hope you are proud
Without a job and still struggling

Not much has changed since you left
Nigeria is ridden with corruption
Insecurity, and death
Many youths graduate
Without a job in sight
They roam a nation that
Pays them no mind

Victor Ansor

The tears of orphans
Have ascended on high
When you talk with Jesus
Please beg him for Nigeria
Tell him to send us help
The last hope of man is none but him

Your son Obong struggles
To keep body and soul
He does odd jobs
Including a transportation business
A risky one at that
Expecting all will be well soon
But despite all, he is determined
Hanging on the hope that never fails
The very hope that has
Kept me going till now
As his character is, which you know
Humble and sincere a man he is
Always looking for the welfare of others
Constantly keeping
Contact with his siblings
Ready to help whenever called upon.

Mama, I know it will be surprising
To know that Kokoete is married
Not just married but blessed
With two children

A Letter To My Late Mom

The first was born on October,
Am yet to be told the month of the second
What? You will say but hold your breath
I have gist for you
His wife had miscarried
The first she was pregnant
Don't know if this would have happened
If you were here
A boy he still is but does not see it
Very stubborn, just the way you left him
He jumped into marriage
Before he was due
Now the burden of marriage
Has weighed down on him
If you see Kokoete
You will but cry
Oh, how it turns out
When a mother is not there
Cloaked in controversy, the marriage was
Now there is nothing we can do, but pray

Kokoete is still a pastor
But in a small church
Which he opens after he left the former
Living on paltry allowance
For tendering the sheep
Such a pay that cannot take him anywhere
His job as a Rector was terminated

Victor Ansor

Now at the mercy of favor
He waits upon
His wife is my concern
A stranger she is
Brought into the family
Without proper arrangement
I was not informed
But kept in the dark
I paid a visit
And stumble on the news
That is how I attended
Much to my amazement

The marriage was done in a registry
Very much to my displeasure
Only me and Obong
The siblings represented
Few cousins and friends
Made up the crowd
Others could not make it
Because they were not told
I supported with the little I had
Though I was displeased
What else can I do
A brother he is, I cannot deny him
A mouse with a white tail
So, you will call him
But now he must learn

A Letter To My Late Mom

I believe the hard way
He is a father, the first
Among his brothers
God will see him through
My prayer for him always

Eteka, your last born is still a pride
He graduated with his first degree
I hope you are proud
Far from being a nuisance
A case you know
Responsible he is time can transform
Teaching in police school
A profession he likes
Earning his wages
In a manner most dignified
Drinking and smoking, he but quit
Now ordain a pastor
He preaches on the pulpit
I am so happy for him
I hope you are
It is what you desired for all of us
Eteka is married now mama
He did his wedding last year
I am immensely proud
The last born of the family
Married a beautiful wife
I wish you were here mama

I wish

I remember how stubborn I was, mama
I gave you a headache I mean enough
Once I threw the bible
And walked out on you
But you said something that
Hunts me all my life
"That bible you threw, you will preach it soon"
Those words hurt me
And I regretted the action
And true to your words I now preach it
In books and to anyone
Who gives a listening ear
Words are powerful
Especially that of a mother

Mothers are not to be
Angry at their children
They would act well if they knew better
A teenager's action
Should not bring a curse
For a parent's words
Are immensely powerful
Anything they say is settled in the spirit
They may change the
Course of a child's destiny
Mothers be careful

A Letter To My Late Mom

Do not get angry when
A child misbehaves
Kindly say the right word
And they will come to pass

You are so blessed, mama
To have raised children like us
Your labor is truly not in vain
Seven of us born again, and graduates
None is a concern nor a liability
Always in favor both with God and man
Contributing to society
And advancing the kingdom
A task we took from you
I am amazed

Children can be claimed
To be a blessing only
When they turn out well
Mama, we have not disappointed you
And never will we

God keep you wherever you are
May the chorus of Angels
Keep your heart and soul
May the face of the Almighty
Shine always upon you
May you always be in a green pasture

Victor Ansor

Your soul restores
There shall be no darkness
Wherever you are
The seas shall be calm
And stars ever shining
Till we meet again
That I do not know when

If I was told
One day I will not see you
I would never part nor leave your side
Learning at your feet
As we used to do
Sometimes I blame myself
For not being there
If I was there, you will never have died
That alone breaks my heart, now and then

Mama, the time has come
To tell about myself
But first, let me start
From when I was born

I remember you told me that
I was born by the roadside
On your way to the hospital
I came screaming into this
World at twelve might

A Letter To My Late Mom

Between Saturday and Sunday

You alone a pretty pregnant
Woman in labor at night
Neglected by my father
Who preferred to sleep
Than to take his wife
To the hospital, how cruel
You told me that a farmer
Who returned from farm late
At night helped you in labor
But mama, where did he
Bury my umbilical cord?
I need to know
For therein lies the secret
To my life struggles

For in life mama, I have been
Through a lot
At the verge of a breakthrough
Something always happens
That the expectation collapse
Sending me back to square one
Could this be caused by my birth?
Or where my cord was buried?

Many encounters about my life
That you may never have known

Victor Ansor

Send chills to my bone
Of why my life is different
I have been stagnated, hindered
Oppressed and suppressed
Standing on one spot when
My contemporaries have moved

I seek from the Father of light
What I must do but my
Mind goes back to the beginning
All that I will tell you here mama
Is a tip compare to my misfortunes
For life has not been fair if not for Jesus
This letter will reveal but a little
As I begin to remember

Much has happened
I do not know where to start
Since you left
Sometimes I have the urge
To go to your grave
To shout your name
If you will hear and wake
Life without you is hard, mama
I will always love you
I cross my heart

A Letter To My Late Mom

After your burial, life was tough
With nowhere to go
Nor anyone to turn to for help
Family members, their houses they went
We were left alone
With no one to care
All the promise from relatives
Were lip service
A penny we did not see
Nor their faces behold

We all stayed together in the house
After the burial
Consoling one another
And asking what next
None with money or plan
We were confused
Who will support or stand by us?
What should we do the sibling asked?

They looked at me for
Answers as the eldest son
With nothing to say or do
They look disappointed
The pain in their eyes
Were clear as crystal
I walked to the kitchen
To look for food

Victor Ansor

For not eating well
Through the event
But more because of my inability
To help the family
I felt as if I was a big disappointment
For now, is the time to show
My manhood
To provide and protect
As I open the pot
I broke down and wept
Wept till my whole body trembled

The siblings rushed in and console
Please do not weep brother
You are our strength
God will see us through we bet He will
Gather yourself and do not let us down
For mama is with us now and always
With these words, I kept my calm
But the broken heart has refused to mend

You see, to be a man is not
In words but works
To take responsibility and care
For those under your wings
And failure to provide
For your family is better if
You were not born a man

A Letter To My Late Mom

Be a man when needed and
Your glory will never fade
Neither will you be forgotten
For the holy scripture says
"That a man who cannot provide
For members of his household
Is worse than an infidel"
My heart broke because
When I was needed
I was incompetent
So, I felt less of a man
And broke down in tears

After this, I left Calabar
And went back to Abuja
I left my siblings alone
Without a dime
Not knowing how they will survive
I left them not knowing
When I will see them again
Or what will happen to them
The fresh tears of this moment
Roll down my eyes right now
As I remember the feeling
Of leaving my young
Brothers and sister alone
Without help

Victor Ansor

Oh, help me father for my
Failure of the past
This makes me swear
That what I couldn't do
For you mama, I will do for them
To erase the past and make it
Clean of the dirt that dotted my path

Leaving Calabar to the unknown
With no house, I can call my own
With a torn pocket a bent shoe
And a bleeding heart
That refuse to heal
I vowed to succeed
Despite the odds
To make it in life, I must be a man

Getting back to Abuja
The struggle continued
I postpone my pageant
Because of your burial
A month ahead
Contrary to it season
With tears in my eyes
I went from place to place
Seeking for sponsors
To help host the event
I got a few and decided to continue

A Letter To My Late Mom

I fixed date and got a venue

The preparation was high
But it was against the time
Finally, with God's help
The event was held
Many said I should cancel
For the time was past
I stood my ground
And refused to heed

On that day, the hall was full
I crowned a queen
Contrary to popular opinion
It was a night I will never forget
I guess you were there
To guide me through
For who crowns a Valentine queen in March?
I must ask

It is a long road
When you face the world alone
And no one reaches a hand
For you to hold
What I have faced in life
I can never tell it all
I must work hard, so my
Children won't face them

Victor Ansor

I have seen difficulties
That words cannot explain
Yet in all these moments
I knew one thing
That my Father in heaven
Never left me for once

I got to a point
I could not bear any longer
But I thank God
Thought of suicide never crossed my mind
When I see people kill themselves
I think how foolish they are
Whatever makes them do that
Cannot be compare
To what I passed through
Yet still holding on
I am still here mama
I am still standing

The greatest asset in life
Is to have hope
For when all fail
Hope can keep you going
I always believe tomorrow will be better
With hope in mind
I wake to face each day

A Letter To My Late Mom

After the event, life
Returned to normal
With no resource
I did not know what to do
I prayed and prayed
Then decided to act
I got a script
And went into production
An investor showed up
And lend me some money
I shot the movie within a month
And then was done
I paid Nollywood stars
More than I should have
Made lots of mistakes
And one almost cost me my life
The crew I worked with
Were no professionals
All the money I borrowed
Went down the drain

The lender tried to kill me
By God, I escaped
He sent my friends with guns
They planned for me to make a mistake
To show anger or
Aggression when provoked
Then they can shoot me in response

But I don't know what happened
That day, I came in great spirit
Whatever they did, bothered me not
I smiled and greeted everyone
I even bought them drinks
And made jokes that they even laughed
Their plot failed to their
Outer amazement
Thank God, your prayers through
The years have helped

Mama, I remember what you told
Me about having friends
For they can be used against me
This proved to be true
For it was not strangers that tried
To kill me but friends that
I spent time with
They smiled at me with a weapon
Of destruction in their pocked
If not for the unseen Father
And your prayers mama
I would not be around
To represent you on this earth

Mama, I tried so many things
But they seemed not to work
What do I do, I must survive?

A Letter To My Late Mom

A man I am must be responsible
Now I know, every child needs a father
Growing up without one is a bad idea
You played the role of both to us
But a father is needful, I must confess

Absentee fathers constitute a big problem
They brought children
To this world but refuse
To be there for them
Many in prisons and crack houses
Would never be there
If not for absentee fathers

They are not there to guide and protect
To show the boys they will soon be men
To teach them how to love
And take care of the women
To be the first boyfriends
To their daughters
And give them a sense of security
That they may grow to
Respect men, and act well
To be obedient and responsible citizens
Contributing their quota
To make the world a better place
A lot can go wrong
When a father is not there

Victor Ansor

After the movie, I thought
Of what next to do
I wrote to the wife of the president
And she responded
She invited me to the presidential villa
With speed, I went
I know you will smile
While reading this
Remember when I wrote
To the governor's wife
And she responded?
She was always sending for me
Right before your eyes

I have a high calling
You always say
One day I will be highly placed
I hope it comes to pass sooner than later

After presidential visit
I started visiting people of substance
I raised some money
And invested in the beauty pageant
With publicity on national television
The event was broadcasted
Contestants responded in their numbers
I was excited and very determine

A Letter To My Late Mom

On the day of the event
I was arrested and accused falsely
A girl I made queen
Claimed I defrauded her
But was a lie, I did no such thing
Here is what happened, mama
I never hide anything from you
As a queen, she
Contributed some money
To host the children
After sometimes she refused to work
We couldn't bear it anymore
She had to be dethroned
When we started
Promoting the next edition
She was not involved
Disgrace, she went to
The police and lied
Promising them half
The cut of the money
If am arrested
The only way to wipe
Her shame, I think

Mama, can you imagine
I crowned a beauty queen
From the police cell?

Victor Ansor

I directed the pageant on
Phone from the police cell
Till my phone battery went
Dead, then I rested

It was not the same unless
I was present myself
Despite the crowd and dignitaries
It was obvious that the organizer
Himself was not around
The special guest of honor noticing this
Stood up and left in anger
Not only him but with his entourage
It was supposed to be
My most glorious season
But it turned out to be a nightmare
The bank I partnered with got upset
Their brand reputation was at stake
But despite all that
I still thank the Lord
That at least I crowned a queen

After the event, the police let me go
When they found out I was innocent
But not without squeezing
Some money out of me
For bail, they called, though "bail is free"
You know Nigerian police

A Letter To My Late Mom

They don't have a conscience
I was asked to press charges, but I refused
I handed the girl over
To God and moved on

At the police station
Someone from the event
Came and said to me
"You are a great man"
Those words sink deep into my heart
I will never forget

Life was not easy
But I must go on
I lost everything yet again
My only asset was a brand
And I held it close to my heart
Would not let go

I took the queen around
On courtesy visits
The money raised was used
To maintain the office
But part of it to settle me

I found a girl
And decided to marry
I proposed to her, and she accepted

Victor Ansor

I rented an apartment
With hope, I have found a wife
She was incredibly supportive
As well as attractive
But I did not know it was a journey
I will one day regret
The relationship was
Not good at all mama
Fight and quarrel
She brought out the worst in me
Her siblings lived with us
I was insulted and disrespected
Every day of their stay
They talked to me however they like
I was miserable and very frustrated
I loathed my house
My own house, mama
Anytime I attempted
To end the relationship
Her catholic priests will call and beg
Clergymen I held in high esteem
I listened and returned to her
But it was not the kind of life I wish to live

Mama, I saw you suffered
In the hand of a man
I have seen what bad
Marriage looks like

A Letter To My Late Mom

I despise and abhor
Instead of the wrong relationship
I better stay alone
I don't have the heart
To bear such a weight

Then one day, I traveled to Abuja
Before I returned, she had moved out
I knew she had an affair
But I held my peace

You see, mama
This is the mistake most
People make
They keep quiet and stay
On in a wrong relationship
The partner will cheat
And or abuse them
Yet they hang on hoping
All will be well
For in time he or she will change
Or so they think
A partner who cheats will
Always remain a cheat
And the cousin of cheating is lies

The result of staying
In a bad relationship

Victor Ansor

Are regrets
That leaves a bad taste
That lingers for too long
If only the victim comes out alive

When she left, I was heartbroken
The only friend I had
Left unannounced
In my heartbreak
I ran to the church
Seeking the intervention
Of one who knows better

I complained to my pastor
Who listened with great interest
All I wanted was a prayer and blessing
With a prophecy that will bring her back
But all the pastor said calmly was
"Peace be still
Thank the lord that she left
Praise His holy name"
I wonder what sort of pastor he is

I explained again in case
He did not understand
Then he calmed me down
And opened the word
I was amazed at the things he said

A Letter To My Late Mom

"When one door closes,
Others will open in unexpected places"
He paused, looked at me as though
To spiritually dissect my innermost being
And see if those words
Found a proper landing
Then continues
"People leave so others will come
Those who will come
Maybe the ones you were dreaming of"
"Your girl left because she didn't deserve you
She has found her type, and so you must
Let her go in your heart
And new doors will open
Forget about her and move along
Else you won't see the right ones
When they come along"

He went further

"When a new chapter
In the life of a man is open
Old things must be flushed out
For new to enter
You have reached a purging moment
Don't block it with stupid emotion
Trust in God, and do His will
Plan your life

And engage in your business
For surely good things are coming your way
That is far better than what
You thought you had."

Those awesome words of the pastor
Changed my life
My eyes popped opened
As if a scale fell off
I listened to him as if God were speaking
I saw a new chapter of my life
Opened before me
I stood up before the pastor
Beaming with smiles
I saw a future full of promises
I walked out of his office
A different man
With shoulders high
I thanked the heavens
That she had left

On getting home, I prayed
She never returned
For I remember how she took
Me to a juju priest in Seme, her uncle
Who bath me at twelve midnight
Draped in white cloths
After bathing naked in a trench

A Letter To My Late Mom

For she wanted me to prosper
In a diabolical way
This I now remember though I forgot
I was tied with a chicken head
On the forehead
And with many rituals the priest
Performed and asked to sleep
In my sleep, I had a dream
Where her mother questioned
The veracity of the ritual
Very displeased she was in that dream
Only to wake up and disregard
Not knowing in the quest
For wealth, my destiny was truncated
If not for Jesus who came to
The rescue
I would be worse than a destitute
Because of love

So, I sat down and think
Of what next to do
Took up my event proposal
And begin planning for next edition
Few months I had, must act fast
Gather my things
And planned a trip
Must host my next pageant
But not in my country

I had a strong push to go to Ghana
The event was national
I changed to international
I contacted a friend and was ready to go
I traveled to Accra
With extremely high hopes
When I reach Accra, everywhere looked good
Every girl I saw, looked like a model
Mama, Ghana girls are very pretty
Dark skin with incredibly attractive curves
I knelt and thank God, that
I was in the right place

Almost carried away with looks
I chastised myself
Considering my last relationship
I keep focus and went to work

It was not easy breaking through
A foreign country
Indigenes saw me as a threat
A foreigner who wants to take over
With a strange brand

I worked hard till I lost weight
The money I went with got finished
I became stranded

A Letter To My Late Mom

And resorted to begging
A friend I stayed with
Soon changed his mind
When he saw I don't
Have the cash to spend
He became uncomfortable
And began to complain
Everything I did was
Displeasing to him
I prayed and prayed
There seemed to be no answer
One day he threw me out in the street
The only one I knew
What will I do?
Where do I stay, I asked myself?
With nowhere to go, and
Not knowing whom to turn
I took my bag and roam the street

No one took me in, I kept moving on
When night fell
I walked to a barbershop
Thank God I barb there once or twice
So, they knew me, I was no stranger
I beg the owner to allow
Me to keep my bag
I told him my story
He took pity on me

Victor Ansor

With a promise to get a place
And return for my bag

Went out that night
Not knowing what awaits me
I met ladies and asked for help
If they could just take
Me in only for a night
For I was afraid
Ladies are easy and compassionate
They understand very often
More than the men
A woman can take pity and take me in
But my case was different
I don't know why
None accepted nor offered to help
I was surprised unlike Ghana women
Seeing a free man who needed a shelter

A lady told me she could have helped
If she was not living with
A boyfriend at Lapaz
She said there is something about me
That is incomprehensible
That I don't look like someone
Who should ask for help
I turned to God and said
Father, I believe you heard

A Letter To My Late Mom

I told her sometimes are like that
That life is in phases and men are in sizes
The man she sees is passing through a phase
And soon it will be over
I may beg today but tomorrow
I will be the one to give to those who need

You see life is quite
Funny sometimes, mama
It rains situation on whomever it will
The reason we should
Not look down on people
When life treats them bad
For like the weather it can turn swiftly
The one you mock today
May be your helper
A helper you desperately need tomorrow
I did not look like a beggar
I despise begging
But life threw me a punch I couldn't defend
Even my pride as a man was put aside
Just for me to survive

Begging on the street of
Ghana taught me a lesson
That to be great you must learn
Sometimes in prison and

Victor Ansor

Sometimes on the street
In the end, the experience is what matter
If you want to confirm
Ask Joseph or Nelson Mandela
Greatness never drops on the laps
But on a well-prepared man
Who has been on the street of challenges

Every man in the ghetto
Has a drop of greatness
If you see one do not despise
For you never know what awaits them
If those I begged see me now
I will be a wonder to them for real
It was a phase I had to experience
Not proud but happy I passed through

I smile as I write this mama
Remembering how it felt
Like in those situations
I made my bed with hunger and thirst
Exhaustion was my friend
And pain, my neighbor
A constant feeling of despair
And anguish
I sailed the rough sea of life
Through the coast of Ghana
Pirates of suffering pillage and plunder

A Letter To My Late Mom

As a captive, I bend for the whips
Of scourge of sun and dust of the earth
Threatened and condemned
I awaited my sentence
But hope saw me through
My best friend in life
And companion forever
Hope never left but always there

I roamed that night
Till I got to a church
Sat down with the security guard
And began to chat
He asked if it is not late
For me to go home
I told him my situation
He felt sorry for me
And accepted to allow me
To sleep in the church
But that no one should know
Or he will lose his job

I was glad
Finally, I got a place to lay my head
I slept in the church bench for weeks
I believe God was watching
And angels were guarding
His mighty hand kept me

Victor Ansor

Like a mother hen, He protected
Under His pinions, I rested
Cannot remember if I had a dream
But I know God's everlasting
Presence was there with me

I got to the church at eleven pm
And leave at four am
To roam the city
With nowhere to go
I walked ten miles or
More to another church
To take a bath
That was the routine for weeks and more
But in all these I was joyful
It did not bother me nor weigh me down
I prayed every day and asked for help
Help from above is what I needed
Since man has refused to help

Please do not despise the
Homeless on the street
Or the ones you see in the
Subway or under the bridge
Be compassionate and kind
For you don't know who they truly are
Or what made them be there
Instead, pray that you don't

A Letter To My Late Mom

Experience it yourself
For its not easy to be on the street
With nowhere to go

To feed myself I must not steal
So, I go to stations where
Buses load to travel
I helped the passenger load their wares
And help negotiate a
Fair price for their cargo
I carried the load with
Hopes to get paid
Bless their heart, they paid
Some generous and
Some greedy or stingy
All the same, I got paid
With the money I bought clothes
And shoe for a change
I ate once a day
And trek all the way

One day Mma called
And said I am needed
For a family emergency
I asked what about
Only to find out that your
Gratuity has been paid
They paid you a million-plus

Victor Ansor

You made a lot at death more than
When you were alive, mama
You put in so much to
Move the system forward
Yet paid stipends to keep body and soul
You woke up early and returned late
Never miss work nor go late
A hard worker you were mama
What you earn was paid at your death
An unfortunate way to appreciate a worker

I asked Mma to share your money
Among us at her discretion
She did and I got my share
With my portion, I renewed my passport
And hosted my pageant
It wasn't big but I crowned a queen
And so, I will never forget Accra my city

After the pageant
I continued in the church
Found friends who took me in
With a place to live
Life was good
Very devoted I was and still, mama

Started serving in the church cleaning unit
I trekked ten miles every Saturday to

A Letter To My Late Mom

Go and clean the church
When I was too tired, I take the bus
Not afraid of what the conductor will do
I sit and look
When they ask for fare, I said I don't have
Sometimes passengers paid for me
And sometimes they threw me out
But not without a curse or two
It didn't bother me at all
For a *"curse causeless causes, no harm"*
Yet in all these never missed church activities
I grew skinny but not discouraged

One day on March thirty-first
I was alone in a room in Ghana
A house I shared with
Friends who took me in
They asked me to join them for a stroll
I refused
At eight pm, while browsing Facebook
Lying on the floor
I heard people talking inside my stomach
It was loud I heard them

A voice said to me within
Won't you speak what you are hearing?
Immediately I opened my mouth

I began to speak in languages I never knew
The voice said again
Are you going to lie down there?
I jumped on my feet
And continue speaking
In tongues for two hours
Mama, it was the most amazing experience
I ever had
I spoke many languages
Chines, Arabic, and many or so it sounds
At exactly ten pm, I stopped
And wonder what just happened
Then it occurred to me
I have been baptized in the Holy Spirit
Alone in my room
With no pastor praying for me

Since then mama
My life has not been the same
I have great insight into the Bible
I long to pray and study the word
Going to church becomes
A habit and not a struggle
I remember how you used to talk
Me into going to church
It is not like that anymore mama
I seek God by myself not needing help
I wake up and pray every morning

A Letter To My Late Mom

At twelve midnight and five am
I long for his presence and nothing else
Am still serving God
Even till this moment

After that, I moved back to Nigeria
With great confidence
And fearless of the devil
Nothing moves me
Both man and beast
Including demons from hell
I do not give a damn

With a whole new perspective
And a relationship with God
I now know what you knew
I carry God within
I feel so secure
His hand with me and never let go
Providing protecting from every evil

People see me as an orphan
But little they know
That my Father in heaven
Worth more than a million father
When God is your father
You are more than covered
He sees what earthly father cannot see

And give what they cannot give
With this, I am not moved
Because I know *the Lord is my shepherd*
I shall not want

Back to Nigeria
I faced challenges
No money no friend
And nothing to do
My rent was due, and I had no clue
I gave up my apartment and sold my stuff
I traveled to Abuja to stay with a friend
Forgetting that the
Spirit I contacted is still with me
He led me about
To favor and breakthrough
Never stranded, never for once

Started working on the
Next edition of my pageant
Sending out proposal
A method you know
With hope, a sponsor will call
Then I started hearing the voice again
This time it says
"Get back to your father's house"
It speaks right from within me

A Letter To My Late Mom

I have never heard the audible
The audible voice of God
But what I hear is a gentle voice
Speaking quietly from within me
So silent yet very powerful and real
As if someone in front of me is talking
I ignored the voice and
Went about my business
It got so strong
That one day I asked the voice
Why do you want me to
Get back to my father's house?
For your information or in
Case you do not know
I don't know my father and
I do not have his address
I never saw my father
Learned he died when I was young
The voice then told me
The name of my father
He gave me four names
You only told me two, mama
He reminded me of the
Village you said he lived
And promised to direct
Me to his address

Victor Ansor

After a while
When life became tough in Lagos
Not knowing where
The next meal will come
Living with people I
Met on a bus to Lagos
No job, no money and nothing to do
I cried and prayed morning and night
With the hardship
I succumb to the voice
Praying it turns out well for me
For I was at a point in life
Almost to give up

I spent all that I had
With nothing to live on
All friends deserted me, no one to care
I was a nobody, I hide from peers
Ashamed, and frustrated
With hunger and tears
The friends I lived with
Did not understand
You go to church and serve your God
But why is life treating you
Like this, they asked

They cook and eat right Infront of me
With saliva to swallow

A Letter To My Late Mom

While watching them eat
Sometimes with pity, they dish for me
When they are done filling their belly
I smile and thank my God
And accept with joy what they offered

It was not easy mama
It is only sweet to write
And not experienced

Why mama?
Why?
Why do we suffer the way we do?
Many families are not like us
Why do we struggle?
And why did you die?
In poverty and never tasted
The best things in life
What happened that
Our family is like this?
What seed did we sow?
That brought this upon us
This I need answers
I need answers mama

Why do good people suffer?
Why do some eat while
Some go hungry

Victor Ansor

Some have mansions
Some are looking for where to sleep
Is God against us
I doubt He is

What did we do?
To suffer in life
Ask the ancestors from
Your abode in heaven
Let them show you why
And please let me know

I decided to go back to
My father's house
But not without prayers
And hesitation
With no money in hand I prepared
When I was ready money
Came from everywhere
The people I lived with
Gave me to my surprise
They bade me farewell
Good riddance to a pest a
Parasite from nowhere
I guess they thought

When I left them
I did not know where I was going

A Letter To My Late Mom

Only following a voice
And the address he gave
When I got to the village
I pause and think
Why will God send me to the village
Away from town
Am I the lost heir to a throne?
Remembering Nigerian movies, I have watched

I took Okada the local transport
After much thought
Headed straight to my father's house
For destiny awaited me there

When I got there
It was like a dream
I beheld my root
The very soil where I come from
For once in my life, I felt like a man
Never had a father figure
Don't know how it feels like to have a father
But that moment it seems to me
What I lost
Has been fully restored

People looked at me on the bike
Like they knew me
They started following me

Victor Ansor

To where I was going
Yet never been there

I introduced myself to the first elder I saw
I mentioned my father's name
Like the son of the soil
The man looked at me and shake his head
He did not utter a word but began to walk
He beckons on me to follow him
And entered a house and shouted a name
A 90-year-old woman emerged from inside
People started gathering
You know village life
The old woman came out
And started staring at me
Everyone kept quiet
And I was confused
And like magic, she called out my name
A 90-year-old woman
Who never met me
Suddenly know who I am
She has not seen me since I was a baby
Taken by you mama
From my father's house
A thing am grateful you did
Although every son needs his father

A Letter To My Late Mom

There was a free flow of emotion
Everyone began to cry
Like a prodigal son
I returned
Only this was never the fault of mine

That was when I knew
I have stepbrothers and sisters
Brother and sisters, I never knew existed
They were informed of my return
The whole family was aware
Calls came from everywhere
I was welcomed with pomp and pageantry
For the first time in my life
I felt I have a family
What could be more sublime in life
Than the feeling of discovering one's root
You never for once thought you have

Life began to take shape
I went to live with my stepsister

So much happened, mama
Since you left
How time flies you will say
Just like yesterday
The memory still lingers

Victor Ansor

Oh, how I miss you
My mother my angel
Tears of anguish
Of sorrow and pain
I miss you so much
Words cannot explain
In life, you were tender and kind
A rare gem and precious you were
Not every woman is a mother

It is not having children from the
Womb that makes one a mother
It is a loving and caring heart
That makes a mother
Like an angel, you were sent from above
May God keep you forever shining
Like the brightest star
We see in the sky
Ever shining
Ever smiling

You showed us the right path
And taught us the right things
Correcting with love
Whenever we go wrong
Always guiding
Like a mother hen
Ready to sacrifice

A Letter To My Late Mom

For us to live

I remember when we had nothing
Seven of us and you make eight
Life was tight
With help from nowhere
You returned one day
From work with news
Eager our eyes were
Looking at your hands
Wondering why no groceries
Since the month has ended

You broke the news
You were not paid
Excuse from the government
The month pay was not available
With sadness, we wonder
Anxious and waiting
What shall we eat?

With a coin in hand, you sent for corn
Two cups of corn we were to share
I cried and wailed
And filled with agony
How can we share
Some grains of corn

Victor Ansor

I was hungry and needed to eat
What shall we do?
Oh, what a life
I saw the pain in your eyes
My heart sank
As young as I was
I knew you were in tears
Sobbing silently beneath the smile
You sacrificed your corn for me to eat
And silently walked to your room
And knelt beside the bed
Pouring your heart
To the power above
I felt so bad at what I saw
I swore to make it in life
Just to take care of you
A promise I have not fulfilled
Time has not been kind
For me to keep the vow
Oh, how I wish you were alive
It hurt me a lot
It hurt me, mama,

One day you returned home
With bags of groceries
We started jumping
And singing at the same time
Praising the lord

A Letter To My Late Mom

For divine provision
I unpacked the bag
And there behold
A full chicken in all its glory
With tomatoes and rice
A delicacy we have not tasted for long
I began to sing and dance for joy
When I was done you called me aside
Put on your cloth
You commanded
That am going on an errand
Wondering where that might be
I obeyed

You packaged the chicken, tomatoes, and rice
Instructing I should take it to the pastor
What? I screamed
Much to my dismay
You simply said a word I will never forget
It is more blessed to give than to receive
We are fortunate and blessed
But don't know if the pastor
And his family have ought to eat
We got some, so we must give the best
And so, I took the journey
With tears in my eyes
Remembering all the past days
We had nothing to eat

Victor Ansor

I walked a mile to the pastor's house
When I got there, I saw sad faces
Wondering what is wrong
In my pastor's house
Thinking there was mourning or so

Greeting the pastor
I mentioned my mother
Delivering the package beneath his feet
He wondered what that was and looked
I asked him to open
And then continue to watch
He looked at it and smile a bit
What for he questioned
With great amazement
A gift from my mother
I said to him
Please accept from
The hand of my mother
The pastor looked at me
Almost shedding tears
He called his wife
And broke the news
We have what to eat
Oh, bless the lord
The children came and gather
Jumping for joy
I was amazed

A Letter To My Late Mom

My tears turned to joy
At what I saw
The pastor told me what
I will never forget
You saved us from hunger
He said
May the Lord bless your mother
Right before you came
We held a prayer
Asking the Lord to provide for us
Your mother is an angel
I must confess
May the Lord continue to bless her
Now and forever

I left that house
Not the way I went
Asking myself
How did mama know?
I was filled with joy
And began to sing
When I told you the story
You were so excited
But you did not know
The lesson I learned
That was the day I knew
The power of giving

Victor Ansor

You touched many lives
I must confess
It takes a mother to do what you did
Oh, how I wish you are still here

I remember one day
When you took me to the market
I was impatient trying to cross the road
Because the cars refused to stop for us
And was taking too long
You told me what I will never forget
It is better to be late
Than to be the late
For the first time, I heard those words
It sunk deep into me
And stayed in my heart
I must learn to be patient
And not be in a hurry
A virtue
I am yet to fully cultivate

I know you will smile
When you read this
Memories of old will flash
Through your mind
For a lot happened
Through your lifetime on earth

A Letter To My Late Mom

I wish you could whisper to me
From where you are
Saying those things not lawful for human
To guide me and show me the way
For a spirit you are now, a spirit indeed
Your flesh in the grave where we laid
Resting till the end of time
Or the trumpet sound

Life is different now mama
I need a mother
To advise and direct
I look to the heavens
From where comes my help every day
If not for God I would have long gone
Temptations and trails
Upon me, they come
But God my father
Is always there to help
He never left mama, he never left

Now I remember mama
All that I did to you
I did not regard nor heed your advice
Stubborn, arrogant, and disrespectful
A son I was
If only I listened, life would be different
The things I rejected

Victor Ansor

Need I most now
Things I was warned against
Now my face they stare
I thought I knew better
How stupid I now feel

Oh, what a mother you truly were
Every child must listen to their mother
For there lies wisdom, long life, and peace
I did not know, now I wish I knew

The scripture says:
"Children obey your parent
For this is right
Honor your father and mother
So that it may be well with you"
I violated this golden rule
Only ask God for mercy

Mama, I want to tell you
What you missed
History was made
Right after you died
An event that changed
The world forever
A black man became
The president of America
An impossible became possible

A Letter To My Late Mom

His name is Barrack Obama
From Kenya they said
He is an inspiration to
Both Black and White
That dreams can come true
If only you believe
He was voted into
Power by the majority
He did two terms in office
And impress the world
A fine man with one wife, two
Daughters, and two dogs
An exceptionally beautiful
Family I must confess
A true picture of the American dream
Without the white picket fence

Oh, I wish you experienced it
For it happened a year after you left
I remember you called
Me one day from sleep
To watch the wedding of Princess Diana
You were intrigued
Glowing and giggling at every turn
If only you stayed a bit longer
You would have been part of history
History written in black
Engraved on the paving of rocks

Victor Ansor

The rock of African descent
On Kenya's threshold

How are you doing over there, mama
What are your daily activities like?
Have you seen our family lineage?
If yes
Ask them questions
Let them tell you what they did
The seed they sowed
That has germinated
Through generations
Ask them why other families
Prosper and ours not
Why we suffer and others don't
Let them tell you the truth
Truth only you can share with me
For every family has a history
Ours is not a pleasant one
What covenant they made
By blood or oath
That keeps our women unmarried or late
The men suffer with no headway
Why we cannot have
Obama in our bloodline
To make history and shake the world
If not that we found Jesus
Our end would have been

A Letter To My Late Mom

Worse than a dog's

Mama, ask them
For we need answers here on earth
To rewrite our history
And change our course
For a sad one we have
And must change
Get these answers mama
Please get them

So much has happened since you left
The world has turned upside down
Climate change, suicide bombing
And dangerous diseases
Idiots and crazy men becoming
Leaders of nations
Wars, wildfire, and conflicts
That claims many lives
There are more refugees than
Free people in some regions
Ebola, Coronavirus, Legionnaires
And Zika diseases and much more
Has ravaged the earth
No more white Christmas in New York
Because of climate change
Can you imagine

Victor Ansor

I fear that snow and bitter cold
May soon hit Nigeria
And other African countries
Not ruling out the
Possibility of wildfire
If it happens, it will be a great disaster
For there is no leadership in Nigeria
A broken system and failed government
The reason we cry to God to send help

Nigeria is like a country under siege
Curse with bad leaders and the likes
We have morons as presidents
The worst of them on the seat
This very moment

When you were here
It was a bit better
Close to steady electricity
It was not an issue
Things were a bit cheap
The reason why we did not die
Now it is not like that mama
There is so much suffering
Difficult to get by
No job, no money
People resort to dubious life
Kidnaping is near a legitimate business

A Letter To My Late Mom

The police-involved
They act as an informant
Expecting a share
Politicians do not care anymore
Stealing the nation blind
Women resort to prostitution
To keep body and soul
Politics is regarded as a business
Not governance
Violence and conflict
A normal routine

Churches are full
And people are praying
Yet answers seem far from coming to us

Nigeria is so fragmented
Divided between ethnic
And religious lines
It is easy to bring peace
In the middle east
Than to bring all
Nigerians into one agreement
There is no unity in Nigeria
A mistake and unjust marriage
Caused by Lord Lugard
With a stroke of a pen
He married the North and the South

Victor Ansor

We were not meant to
Be one country, mama
This marriage is destroying us
How can we divorce?

Ask Jesus for the way forward
The way forward for Nigeria my country
I love Nigeria mama
Every day I weep for her redemption
Tell Jesus to send a Daniel
For we need a leader
We need it now

Yet I cry out for you mama
My heart bleeds day and night
Every thought of you makes my heart sink
My love for you will never die
When I see old grey hair women
I wish mine was alive just like that
I cannot bear to see a ninety or a hundred
But wonder why mine was cut at her prime

Why did you die mama, why?
You promised to be there for all time
But failed to keep your promise to us

Wiping my tears
And in whispers

A Letter To My Late Mom

I want to ask you a
Private question mama
Have you seen my
Children in heaven for real?
They are many I know
You are surprised
Many and from different mothers
I sowed my wild oats in
A wild way indeed
Do not blame me for it, mama, please don't
A young man without a father
What did you expect when left alone?
I plunder and plowed
Pleasured, I took a dive
The result is what you see
Do not be mad at me mama, don't be

I know you are surprised yet happy
Every mother yearns for grandchildren
Now you have yours
And in a better place
They keep you company
And busy I believe.
What are their names?
Can you tell me?
How grown are there?
I need pictures
Do they miss me or talk about me?

Did they start school or finished?
I need to know

What do you every day?
I hear there is no night in heaven
If so, when do you sleep
Or do you at all?
Aside from your grandchildren,
Have you seen my
Sister that passed on?
How is she doing?
She must be grown woman by now
Beautiful as you described
I hope the guys in heaven
Don't bother her
Else I will take it personal

Do you have an audience with Jesus?
How is he like
Please send me pictures
Or selfie in your reply

My journey has been a long one mama
Few months after I started
Living with my stepsister
The voice asked me to leave
For film school abroad, I obeyed

A Letter To My Late Mom

I live in America now mama
In New York to be specific
The first time I came
I ran back to Nigeria
The voice asked me
What I am doing there
As soon as I landed in
Lagos airport
It dawns on me that
I made a mistake
The voice promised to
Take me back to America
It did

Since then mama, I live in New York
It is the most beautiful
Place on earth thus far
Life is fast and expensive yet
Intriguing and fabulous
It is mesmerizing and far from
Any experience one may have
In Nigeria
A mixture of old and modern
A city of many bridges, tunnels
And underground railroads
A magnificent and awe-inspiring city
The buildings are closely built
There is no space between them

Isn't that interesting mama?
I see it as a good thing
It saves people from
Fighting over land space

From my description mama
You may come to visit in the spirit
But you need to be flesh and blood
To feel it and enjoy it
To experience the New York police
Lurk around in corners like Hyenas
Ready to pound on you with
Tickets and summons, like candy
To stop and frisk if
Your color looks different
Or appear to be suspicious
Under their radar
You wouldn't have a problem
With the color issue
Since you were White
But this is a different world
Entirely from what you know, mama

I Live in Queens mama
They do not throw dirt on the street
Like in the movie "Coming to America"
Black people don't steal stranger's luggage
That was a bad representation

A Letter To My Late Mom

Of Black people's character
I know we are not perfect
But it is not that bad

New York is accommodating
Despite the impatience of its residents
The easiest place to make money on earth
But the easiest place to spend all income
On vanities and bills

Money does not grow on trees
And you cannot pick them
On the street, as we thought, mama
Hard work procures wealth here
And the only way to make it
Is to defy the cold and go to work
People work many jobs just to
Make ends meet
A lazy person cannot survive here
For hunger will kill without mercy

Although they are advanced
Yet not that perfect, mama
They also have bad roads
Poor people and beggars
That sometimes I thought
I am in Nigeria
But one thing I love is that

Victor Ansor

They listen to citizens complain
And have a high maintenance culture
A thing we lack that brings decay

Within seven years of my stay
In New York mama
I got all the Degree I needed
And graduated Magna Cum Laude
I am also a published author
And a professional photographer
All that I lost in Nigeria
God gave me back In the United States

I must say, mama, that I have
Achieved the American dream
For a true American dream is far from
A family, dog, and white picket fence
When you achieve what you
Could not in your country
That becomes the American dream
Any level of success achieved in
America is the American dream

God bless America
For allowing me to gain back what I lost
For embracing an immigrant like me
Accepting me into the system
And helping an orphan like

A Letter To My Late Mom

Me to stand on my feet
I owe it all to you America
God bless you

It is ignorance and gross
Stupidity to think that
Immigrants are the problem
A narrative coin by wicked
And hateful politicians
Who decides to use such to
Gain political ascendency
I have seen in all my years
In this great country
That diversity is the root
Cause of its supremacy
Any contrary opinion is ignorance

I remember when you told me one day
That if you had money
You will send me to America to study
Well, mama, I am here today
Your wish came true
The reason why we should be mindful
What we wish for

I did not expect to be where
I am today mama
Nor achieve all that I have today

Victor Ansor

God has been faithful
The heavens have been good to me
My tears have been wiped
And sorrow taken away
An orphan on earth
Once homeless and famished
Living as a prince

I have no need now mama
Only to fulfill my destiny
To be a blessing
And help others
My heart cry every day
And all that I pray for

Mama, the kind of favor I have
Here in America is amazing
Would you believe that my first month
In New York, a woman saw me on the
Train and gave me five hundred dollars
She said God told her to do it
So, she said to God if you truly
Want me to give the money
Bring him back on this same train
Wearing the same cloth and
Hanging the same bag
Three days later I was on the
Same train wearing the same

A Letter To My Late Mom

Cloth and hanging the same bag
And she gave me the money

A man also gave me a house
To live free for five years without
Paying a dime
This among other favors I received
I believe your kindness to
Strangers and prayers
Procure me these blessings
For I remember how you took
Care of orphans and treated
Our house helps better than us
We are reaping the harvest
Of your kindness, mama

The world will soon end mama
And many do not know
All the bible prophecies
Are getting fulfilled
New diseases and natural disaster
Political instability and social disorder
Hunger and war with rumors of war
Anxiety and great
Perplexity the earth visited
Everything is leading to
A final breakdown
I wish all humanity knows

Victor Ansor

This and run to God

I ask God every day
What part I should play
I sense that I was born
For such a time as this
But what should I do?
Is there a role for me
This end-time I ask?
Oh, how I wish it is
Revealed to me now

I remember the dream
I had when I was a boy
How I preached by the Calabar
River with an open bible in hand
The bible was opened to
Mathew twenty-four
The topic was
"Many are called but few are chosen"
When I check there was no correlation
A large brick was brought by someone
In the crowd and I was asked
To stand on while preaching
I stood on it and continue preaching
When I woke up, I told you
You smiled and said
That Great things await

A Letter To My Late Mom

Me in the future
I don't know what it means
I still do not know

I desire to run for office
To be the president of my great country
To end the hunger and corruption
That has plagued us for a long time
This desire keeps growing every day
I yearn to help my people
To bring peace and
Prosperity that all cry for
To stop the menace that
Causes people to run abroad
To use our vast resources and change lives

Mama, please I need your help
Read this letter to Jesus I beg you
Not everything but this very part
He does not need to hear about
My vanities, sins, and pleasure
Don't allow him to read for himself
Only the part of my political interest

As the son of God
I know he will be intrigued
He might send an angel
To fulfill this dream

Please do this for me and all Nigerians
For Nigeria needs a leader of integrity
Who will shun bribery and
Execute judgment and justice
Who will plead the cause of
The fatherless and the widows
A man of insight and understanding
With vision and a mission
Who will steer the nation
To it ordain greatness

Nigeria is a laughingstock in
The committee of nations
We are mocked and ridiculed
A nation leaderless and fractured
Oh, mama tell Jesus he needs to hear

Mama, I remember when
I was eleven years old
You planned to leave your Abusive
Husband my stepdad
A sneaky plan I did not understand
You asked me to take permission
In school and come home at ten
I was afraid of the school principal
And delayed
Two hours later after I ran home
You had packed out and

A Letter To My Late Mom

Moved all your belonging
The neighbors told me
Where to find you
I was heartbroken
Because I failed you

You were mad at me and said
"Papa, I trusted you and
You disappointed me"
I begged for forgiveness yet
Cannot forgive myself
I felt like the man who could not
Be there when you
Needed me the most
All my life I have been
Trying to fill that gap
But nothing can undo an error made
I plead for mercy

Mama, there are many times
I would have died
But the unseen father
Delivered me and kept me
Some I told you but many
I kept to myself

The invisible hand that pushed me
From my back when

Victor Ansor

I almost fell into the crocodile
Infested river while trying to fish

The bus that stopped instantly
From falling into a cliff
When I shouted the blood of Jesus

When I miraculously woke
Up twenty-four hours
After a doctor injected
Me for kidney diseases
And all my bones got weak and numb

A mobile policeman
Who cocked his gun to
Shoot me simply because I
Questioned his actions at a function

The ghastly accident I had
And came out unscratched
while the car got totaled

These among others that you
May not know about
But the Lord is my shepherd
And will continue to be

A Letter To My Late Mom

My life has been full of miracles
It baffles me how I made it alive till now
The enemy tried to snuff
The life out of me, but God refused
A battle ongoing but
My name is a winner

I remember you said that I died
Had a severe fever as a baby
You took me to the hospital
Leaving me to go and buy food
On your return, you asked for me
The nurses said that I died
So, they cover my body
And put me among the dead
At the back of the hospital
You shouted that I am not dead
Why put my baby among the dead?
And demanded to see my dead body
They took you outside where I was kept
There I lay covered head to toe
You took me and put on your back
With tears and cry, you walked
Mama, you walked around the hospital
Weeping and calling on the Father above
They thought you were crazy
But some situation calls for crazy faith
So, on the seven times
The heavens heard and I sneezed

Victor Ansor

I sneezed out the sting of dead
And came back to life

Your love brought me back mama
God does not deny the cry of a mother
For a mother's love is stronger than death

The hospital erupted with joy
Seeing a boy brought back to life
He was dead and now alive
The news spread and awe fell
You caused a miracle that never happened
Because of the love you have
For your son
So, I lived and refuse to die
For your love for me is stronger
I kept the story in my heart
Pondering on it now and then
I will forever love you

Mama, I have so much respect for
You aside the love
How you were able to carry through
Till the end of life
In poverty yet dignified
In need yet never begged
A single mother yet chastised
Many men came but you refused

A Letter To My Late Mom

The customs officer who bothered you
He claimed you are his wife
He promised to accept
Us all just to marry you
You refused though he had money
He had the money and love to give us all
But because of me, you said no
And told me that you don't
Want anyone to come
And mistreat me considering
My former stepdad

Thank God mama we were
Not born in America
Only in Nigeria would that happen
To keep seven children in
One room with poor income
To feed sometimes once a day and a baby
They would have taken us from you
Maybe never to see again

We all should be proud
Where we come from
Many things we take for granted
Should be thankful
For our life is designed
By an unseen hand
Who knows tomorrow
And fix us appropriately

Victor Ansor

It may have been hard
Yet we survived
We made it through the toil
And left no one behind only you mama
Buried in the sand of conflict
We sing the anthem
Never to let go no
Matter where we are
For good soldiers don't forget a comrade
Only this time you were our captain

Adieu mama adieu
For gracious is the
Sight that beholds you
And pleasant indeed
A woman most beautiful and elegant
More organized and good character
Loved by all and plenteous in good
The world has missed
And misses a gem
A true reflection of a virtuous woman
Who loved her children above herself
You will never die in my heart
That I promise
To live always as long as I breath
I will always love and forever miss you
The world may not know you

A Letter To My Late Mom

But your children do
That is enough if accompanied by love
You are our champion
May God be with you

Mama, do you remember
When you traveled
To go and give birth to our last born
When your husband almost kill me?
Now let me tell you
I was seriously abused
If in America, I would
Have reported him
Report to the authorities
If the status of limitation does not expire
He abused me among others

I was sexually molested but not by him
His was beating and
Psychological abuse
He used the heel of your
Shoe to cut my head
The scare is still there as evidence
He one day asked
Me to eat a full pot of rice
Rice cooked for five
I finished at once
My stomach bulged

Victor Ansor

I thought I would die
It's a miracle I made it alive

He one day asked me to
Eat from the dumpsite
Food spoiled and thrown away
Forced to eat with all the germs
The aim was for me to
Die but God kept me
I am still alive though he is gone

Mama, concerning another abuse
I will tell you and only for your ear
Please don't tell Jesus nor
The angels in heaven
They are for your ears
And your ears alone

A man in the market you use to send me
A boy I was and very vulnerable
To buy yams he smiled at me
Promise to give free if
He touches my thing
I laughed and thought a joke
He said I should come
And not be afraid

A Letter To My Late Mom

With a promise for free yam
I approach in fear
He touched and squeezed
And looked fulfilled
He gave me the yam
And ask to come back
Yam is here if only I touch
I was amazed at how simple it was
But ashamed so I conceal the matter

I use the money for the yam
To buy other things
When you asked me where
I got the money from
I lied that I got a good bargain
I have kept this secret till now mama
Please forgive me for not telling you

I was abused because of money
Poverty is a curse that leads to many
I tasted mine thank God
I did not stay there

Mothers talk with your sons
About who touches them inappropriately
More attention has been given
To girls being abused but
We forget that boys are also

Victor Ansor

Very vulnerable and susceptible
To abuse, and parents
Mind where your children
Go, and ask them questions regularly
For in this you might be
Surprised at what you find

No one has an excuse to
Stay where they are
Maybe I am different but
Do not see an excuse
Shake up the past and move along
Change the course and chart a new
Do not dwell in it don't sleep on it
It should not define you no not at all

Always surprise when
I see people complaining
That abuse changes their lives
It made them turn out
Bad instead of good
I thought about how that is
Considering my experiences
I don't have answers but to keep silence

I of yesterday is not me of today
I don't let anything define
Me or weigh me down

A Letter To My Late Mom

For the fact, I wake up
Is a new day for me
The past is gone a new day begins
I face each day as
Though a new beginning
With confidence, I attack with all vigor
Giving my best and
Drowning yesterday
I am a man made of today

Even God love men of courage
And courage is facing each day afront
As in battle not thinking of defeat
For warriors are born of sweat and blood

Hope and courage when married together
Can create a man not seen before

Do not dwell on yesterday
Whether good or bad
For our greatest undoing
Is the day long gone

I am here, still here mama
In America, the land of the free
Though that freedom is
Facing a serious challenge
Time will tell and the

Victor Ansor

Next letter will explain

I arrived at this shore broke and battered
With dreams and hope, I continue to sail
The rough waters of the Americas I sail
Each day pass with more
Promise in sight, I sail
That one day I will land on
The shore of discovery
A land paved with milk and honey

I have arrived although on the shore
With much assurance from treasures I found
The chest of wealth inland awaits
I will fight with all courage and bravery
Spilling and cutting my way to the top
On this glorious land that Columbus found
I will make my mark or so I dream

Mama, it is time to talk about you
To say the thing kept for ages
To reveal and to question with love at heart
I have so much to talk about you mama

What were you thinking
I must ask
Walking out of abusive marriage with

A Letter To My Late Mom

Seven children and small income?
I respect that action
For it is unheard of in our culture
That a woman leaves a marriage
And more so with the children
You were not selfish, you left
With your children
Not thinking how you will survive

But

Why did you stay through
All those years of abuse?
I saw how your husband
Treated you so badly
Yet you endured and kept
Silence and stayed on
He almost killed you
This I saw many times
I know you will be surprised
That I remember them

Once You and stepdad were quarreling
It got so intense that we all
Were crying in another room
You alone with the newborn baby
In the room with him
He locked the room and

Victor Ansor

The baby was crying so loud
Maybe the baby's spirit knew
Something terrible was about to happen
I was so afraid that he will kill you
He talked so loud beneath
His drunken stupor
He then brought out his sword and
Threatened to cut you in pieces
I know you will remember that day

You shouted and the neighbors came out
One of the neighbors got so angry
And wanted to fight him
They asked you to come out of
The room to their house
You refused and said
If he wants to kill you let him go ahead
If that will satisfy him
You sounded so bold and unshaken
I was afraid to my bone
Even right now writing this letter
The feeling still came back
It was one of the most dreadful
Moments of my life
That night I couldn't sleep
I thought he will kill you or me
But you slept in the same room with him

A Letter To My Late Mom

Mama, marriage is supposed to be
A beautiful thing but when
Partners turn violent and terrorists
In their own home, that marriage
Has lost its essence
Marriage should exist with
Love and mutual respect
Each looking out for each other
And remaining best friends for life

Mama why did you have such
Misfortune with men
Maybe if you tell me
I might warn others
A beautiful woman like you
Got entangled with evil men

Why did that happen?
Who caused it or what caused it?
You have answers now that you are a spirit
For spirits knows better than the living

Why were you so unlucky?
Is it caused by our ancestors?
Is it a cursed placed on our family?
I have not seen any enviable
Marriage in the family
There is no marriage void of trouble
Why is that mama?

Victor Ansor

Grandma passed on before you
So, ask her if she is in heaven
Get all the information and pass on to me
For such a marriage as ours, I do not desire
Why things went the way they did
I need to know

Every day was quarreling no peace at all
When stepdad is not home joy returns
At the sound of his bike
We ran seven ways
Each take position for terror returns
He was unfriendly and cruel to the core
Drunk always and fighting with you
Who in his right sense fight
A woman as beautiful as you?
Yet he brought shame on us
A thing disdain

You were an epitome of beauty
I still remember
With long black hair cut every year
You looked whiter than
The White man indeed
Many said you were from the water spirit
Is it true? I know you will laugh
You were so beautiful

A Letter To My Late Mom

The envy of all
One a night in shiny armor
Your feet will sweep
Yet a man undeserving abused and shamed
Treated with dishonor, disrespected and curse
I forgive him
Oh God help me to forgive

Mama, do you still cut your hair?
In heaven, as you used to do yearly
Now you would have made money with it
African women especially Nigerians
Are so fascinated with
Barbie looking kind of hair
They think it makes them beautiful
How dumb that is
I think they lack identity that is why
They go looking from White folks
Knowing who you are and
Embracing your identity
Is the best expression
Of self, Black people need to know this

Your passing reveal so much to me
Your heart was tender though determined
With years of rubbing it lost it thread
Wounded at the end could not bear at all
It gave up such a beautiful soul
The world has lost a gem

Victor Ansor

I remember how you bought
Things in stepdad's name
Honor him before all the neighbors
From fridge to TV to couch and food
He looked responsible when visitors arrive
You put his name on the receipt
To pretend he owned them
Bought a land to build him a house
All that he refused to see
But let liquor and wickedness lead him astray

A man deserving you missed, mama
I wish you did not marry
You will still be alive
He caused your death for this I am sure
Took you out when life just began
I know you will look
Down and feel my pain
The anguish in my heart
For remembering all these
Time flies and so do memories
But mine lingers and it lingers for long

On Christmas, you bought us clothes
The food the drinks all came from you
He prides himself a man yet denied his duty
On concubines his income spent

A Letter To My Late Mom

He brought one of them home one day
I saw the hidden tears and pain in your eyes
A thing so fresh in my memory till now
They threatened you and laughed at you

Fresh tears of this memory
From my eyes, they flow
They mocked and laughed and shouted
Eat your food and drown your drinks
Tempted you in your house
In front of your children
A quiet woman you were
With no voice at all
You kept the pain and left for church
It cannot happen now, mama
They are so lucky
I would have been the man you never had
To defend your honor, and stand for you
It hurt me, mama
To remember all these

We are from a family that has no love
No unity and very selfish
No one is there for one another at all
I don't think others are
Like us or maybe they are
Everyone knew what happened
Yet none came to the rescue

Victor Ansor

Seven children and a single mom
No one gave to us
No family member cared
In hunger and thirst
They turned their back
But you still send them
Christmas and Easter gifts
With a heart of stone, they
Stretch their filthy hands and collect

I remember all that happened
As we grew, mama
I can narrate them with great accuracy
Very observant and attention to details
I kept all that happened in my heart till now

There is no love in the world today
Not a single drop since you left
Oh, mama, I have been betrayed
By people, I love and hold dear
Stabbed a thousand times
With wounds so deep
Not from foes but friends and lovers
And people I never thought will turn on me
My heart bleeds and tears distill

The world is cruel mama
I can only bare my heart to you

A Letter To My Late Mom

Not others who will use it against me
A trade man has mastered

My heart's been broken in pieces
Again, and again
I trust no one
I am alone
Very much alone
Outside a gathering
I shrink back to the shell
I know too many people
A man of the people
But alone in the crowd

My shell is my world
I don't know who to trust
In this world I am alone
My heart is heavy
My tongue overwhelmed
So much to say, no book can contain
To describe in detail
The plight of an orphan
Oh, what a world you left behind mama

My eyes are wet and filled with tears
My heart heavy with drops of water
I pity the woman I might call a wife
For I have no trust, no

Victor Ansor

Trust left for her, mama
For if man to man has been unjust
Show me the man that I can trust
I have given my heart to many
But burnt many times therefore I shrink
And trust left through the back door
Never to return

I don't have a father or
Someone to talk to that will understand
I don't want to talk to a friend or a pastor
Who can easily use me to preach
In the heat of a sermon
I cannot talk to a psychologist
Who can't be trusted these days
I need a father to express myself
For my heart is full and nowhere to empty

The best things in life they say are free
The air we breathe and love we give
The later so costly and costly indeed
Love is so expensive
You cannot find where to buy
Even when you have to sell
None deserve to purchase

It hurt to see someone you
Love, turn against you

A Letter To My Late Mom

While still staring you in the face
Stabbing you with a smile
To your outer amazement
So much hatred so much betrayal
Friends turn foes, enemies abound
When I thought I escape one
Others spring up
Like grass on the sidewalk

The house of God that
Was supposed to be a sanctuary
And succor for the afflicted a
Haven for the oppressed
Have become a den of
Hatred, bitterness and strive
We do not love one another
Even in church

The greatest commandment
Our savior admonished
Love one another
If you claim to love God

If the world hated me
I would bear it mama
But when church members
Hate with such cruelty
Where should I run to?

Victor Ansor

How can you hate
And still, lift up holy hands
Pastors and members none excused
God must be displeased He really is
For He said we should love one another
Even as he loves us
We preach it but don't live it

Pray for me mama, please pray
I feel lonelier in church
Than in the world
Going to church brew
Dread and discomfort
With confidence I hold
My shoulders high
Among the brethren as if all is well

If we Christians know our
Conduct affect others
We would be careful
And act with caution
How can we convert the world?
With hatred in our heart

Mama, please tell Jesus
What is going on in the church
If with mercy he will

A Letter To My Late Mom

Make things right
For in church, members
Need to love one another

If the hallelujah and a
Great thank you, Jesus,
Can be put aside and love return
Heaven will be glad
And souls converted
For the world reads us like newspaper
It is not what we say but what we do

Action speaks louder
And love is attractive
When love takes its proper
Place in the church
Influx of multitude
Will be the new normal
Love is the greatest commandment
Jesus says
Love covers a multitude of sin
If we love, we will not hate
We spend so much time in church
But our lives do not reflect
That we are truly God's children
Pastors fighting with others
And still, climb the altar to minister
Choir leaders holding a grudge

Victor Ansor

And keeping malice yet
Climb the alter to sing
With a show of holiness
Bitterness hatred and anger
Among members reign supreme

Love and humility left the congregation
And pride and envy rule with an iron fist
If you correct a member or leader
They hate you and make sure others do

We preach to convert others
But those that need to be
Converted are we indeed
Our light supposed to shine
For others to see
Like a city on a hill reflecting Christ
But besides us, we
Hold grudge and keep malice
Fellow members do not
Get along with each other
This is a tragedy in the house of God

We have turned the holy sanctuary
Into a house of sin
For the worst sin is the sin of the spirit
That which no one thought really matter
Help pray for me mama

A Letter To My Late Mom

For I am guilty as others

There is so much competition
In the church today
Brothers and sisters in church fighting
And competing to outdo the other
We strive not to please God
But show a fellow member
We are more blessed

The church is now a citadel of competition
We dress and drive just to show off
Give testimonies to spite another
Form cliques and clubs to exclude others
The world is watching
The least we know
Envy and strive has
Overwhelmed the sanctuary
Like in the days of Jesus we buy and sell
Right in the very house of prayer

There are so many churches within a church
The church is more polarized
Than American politics
If we as a church can come together
For love to rule, blessings will descend
And miracles will happen

Victor Ansor

There are no more
Prophecies in church mama
Our sins and actions have
Stayed the heavens
Please tell Jesus to have mercy on us

So much division in the church today
People love the church and not God
You cannot trust a fellow member
If you confide in them
They gossip about you

Hypocrisy, eye service and
Human worship abounds and you
Cannot know who is serving right
Everyone tries to outdo the other
Not so the Lord might be glorified
But just to attract attention
And look like a saint

We leave the church to do
Business with non-believers
We become more comfortable
With the world than in church
It is in the church that we find
Cruel, mean, vindictive
And judgmental people
Church members will condemn
And crucify without mercy

A Letter To My Late Mom

Don't get me wrong mama
They are still a few
Good people like you
With a good heart
But who can find?

For a man's character is not engraved
In his countenance
The heart of men is evil
And desperately wicked
Who can know it?
A friend today can turn
Bitter enemy tomorrow
Trust no one

I wish the will of God can
Be done on earth quickly
As it is in heaven

Nonetheless, it is in the church that
I find peace and often hear God
Going to His sanctuary has
Become a part of me
It makes me wiser
Oh, what a beauty to worship God
In His sanctuary
I cannot avoid

His house because of men
For there I find refuge and strength

Without the church, the world
Will perish and hell descend
You cannot say you are a
Child of God yet forsake His house
The attitude of men should
Not deter us from attending
His sanctuary
The church will continue
To remain a place of covering
Where God's presence
Ever remain to bless the seed of man

Mama, I have been abandoned
And left by many
In this, I learned a valuable lesson
Never to beg people to stay
For those who left were not
Meant to stay with me
My destiny has nothing to
Do with those who left

I have lost so many people I
Thought I will build a life with
But I notice that life becomes
Better without them
This is a great lesson I must confess

A Letter To My Late Mom

Never beg anyone to stay
If they leave, let them go
And you will see your
Destiny open immediately

It hurt losing people
But for a short while
Those meant for you will surely stay
If you force or beg people
They will make your life miserable
This has been proven time and again

Sometimes it is God
That force people to leave
So that our destiny can open up
Begging or forcing them to stay
Is throwing it back to God
That He doesn't know what He is doing

In most cases, we are delayed
And stagnated by people in our lives
The earlier they leave the better for us
They may not be bad people
But their stay only helps block
Us from fulfilling a purpose

Some relationships are a distraction
Organized to frustrate our destiny
There are people we need to let go
For our lives to become better

Mama, you miss a lot
The world has changed
Not the way you left it
It is becoming very interesting
One could not be born at a better time

You did not live to see
And experience Uber
The new mode of transportation
Which I am a part of
I drive Uber and do photography
The means I put
Myself through college
In New York City
How cool is that
Your Uber rating
Would have been high
To reflect your good personality
Soon employers may
Demand Uber ratings
To see how employees'
Fares in the real world

A Letter To My Late Mom

You did not know Amazon
An online store
Where you can buy
Anything except human
Just order and they will
Deliver to your doorstep
I hear the owner is the world richest man

Mama, you did not even
Have a Facebook account
Nor see nasty pictures on Instagram
A place where you find
Naked women at every turn
Not a good place for a man of the spirit

You did not follow people
Who rant their stupid mind on Twitter
A free press that even the poor
Can speak their mind
And government listens

What an interesting world you missed
It hurts that you did not even drive
With GPS and hear a
Woman's voice directs you
Every step of the way
It is mind-boggling, mama
How they did that I cannot even imagine

Mama, Koko posted
Your picture on Facebook
I don't know how many likes you got
But you did not go viral
I'm sorry
Likes on social media matters now mama
Friendship is defined by
How many likes you get
People lose touch with one another
And bury their soul on the internet

I don't know how good you
Are with news over there
Just to let you know that the
Present president of America
Wants to build a wall
To stop people from coming
Into his country
Is that not funny, mama
How can a country build a
Wall at such a time as this?
When better policies are
Needed to steer the world

The universe depends on the
United States for direction
If the leader of the free world

A Letter To My Late Mom

Spend time in wall building
Then disaster and dangerous
Times has visited the earth
For nations don't build walls
But embrace with open
Hands with love for
The destitute of the earth
Who flee their abode in search of help

Do they have walls in Heaven?
If they do, then my mind will calm
For I will know it is a divine agenda
But if no walls in heaven
Invoke the angels to pull
The one here down
Not so miscreants can take advantage
But such revenue channel to help the poor

Mama the woman I want to marry
Is a mystery woman
I love her so much with all my heart
She is the one I love
The type of woman my heart desire
I drive miles to see her
Not quite often
I knew her when I landed
On this shore of treasures
She stole my heart I can't explain

Victor Ansor

I forgive her no matter what she does
No sin greater than my love for her
My love for her is
Unfailing and true
I will do anything to
Make her my wife
If another gets her
I will continue to love
But from a distance
A mystery woman she is mama
She is in my life and she is not
I have her and I don't have
I wish a divine hand
Can put things right
For I long for her above all else

Mama, I don't mean to gossip
But I know a lady in the church choir
Who prefer to sleep with White
Men for money, can you imagine that
She refuses to work and
Earn her pay with dignity
But prefer prostituting with White men
Instead of dignified labor
She thinks nobody knows about it
But before the Father
Everything lays bare
And me, I try to know what's

A Letter To My Late Mom

Going on in my father's house
A talent I acquire from where I cannot tell

I may not work at central intelligence
And may not keep files on everyone
Like the CIA
Yet I seem to have firsthand knowledge
Of everything going on around me
People don't fear God
Anymore, even in church
If you see her sing or hear
Her preach the word
You will think she is a saint
She boasts of paying tithes
With her hard earn money
Not knowing she is simply
Reporting herself to God

Another lady in church
Threw insult at me
She accused me of refusing
To marry despite my age
I don't know what her problem is
Married with a child she won't let me be
I confronted her and ask to stop
Since then, she does
Not talk to me anymore
I don't know what people
Have become these days

Victor Ansor

One cannot find a true friend
People get close for self-interest
And if the interest is
Threatened, they dig a trench
Life has become so unfair

There is a pastor in the church who
Hates me, mama
He can't even bring himself to
Talk to me, he presents himself
To be a saint, one too holy
To behold my person
He has no love in his heart
Towards me, yet preach about love
For God and men always
I wonder with an open mouth when
He mounts the pulpit to talk
About how we should love one another
Yet here I am a man he hates
Oh, what a world of
Hypocrisy we live in

He does not waste time to lift up
Holy hands to show his holiness
Before the people yet a brother
He abhors and cannot even speak to
When Jesus comes
Many will be surprised

A Letter To My Late Mom

I serve under him in
Our local assembly
Faithful, loyal, and committed I am
Two hours before service
I open the door, sweep
Organize and prepare
He comes late sometimes
Though the leader
And walk past a brother
Who keeps the sanctuary
Not a word or blessing
Utter he at anytime
If my reward was to come from him
I will wait a thousand years
A one-man cleaner, technical crew
And doorkeeper yet he cannot see
I am amazed at the heart of men

I Bought a present for one pastor's wife
On Christmas day
Mama, can you imagine that she
Could not even say thank you
The husband sees me and passes by
As if nothing happened
I confronted her to let her
Know I am not happy
For at least she would

Have called and thank
She stopped talking to me

You see we are God's children
And we act like Him
He vows to curse our blessing if we
Fail to give thanks to Him
If God can be displeased
I could too

There is a deacon's wife in church
Who dresses for the club to church
Her outfit paints a prostitute
Yet no one calls her to order
Her voice is the loudest and
She dances more than the birds
She sits right behind the pastors
A stumbling block to non-believers
And new convert
My spirit weeps every time I see
Her in church for it is not normal
The church truly needs revival
The world needs real Christians

A deacon in the church told me
That no matter what I achieve
He will not respect me
Until I get married

A Letter To My Late Mom

Can you believe these church people?
They drink medicine
On another person's headache
They take marriage too seriously

Why do African people
Pay too much attention
To marriage and children
They think marriage and
Children are achievement

Marriage is not an achievement
Having children does not
Constitute a breakthrough
The truth, mama you are aware of
You did not achieve anything
With seven children
You struggle with us in poverty
If that was an achievement or blessing
Please let me know

Children are not a blessing
But a responsibility
They can be called a blessing
Only when they turn out well
If you disagree, take a walk
On the street and you
Will have a change of mind

Victor Ansor

African people bring many
Children into the world
And spend their lives working
To take care of them
They grow older than their age
Their destiny far from fulfillment
In frustration and regret
They force their children
To become what they could not
And so, the trend continues
From generation to generation
None achieve their purpose
None build anything
For the next generation to inherit
They often die and no
One remembers them
In an average grave, they are buried
The children continue
With no inheritance
Many generations pass
With no significant achievement
What a sad story this is

Mama, would you believe that
I have never celebrated my birthday
I tried it once and my friends came
And finished all my food and drinks

A Letter To My Late Mom

And could not even sing a happy birthday
I didn't even cut a cake

Would you also believe that I
Masturbated for so many years?
I went to the beach one day in
Calabar after school and saw a man
Masturbating by the river
I was in junior school three
I went home and tried it
Felt so good and I got addicted
The pleasure turns out bad
After many years, mama
For I lost my hair, my voice grew thin
And so many changes in my
Body yet you didn't even know
I thank God that it did not destroy me
When people say that I am handsome
I wonder what they would have said
If I did not masturbate
For so long in my life

Mama, I have a confession to make
The twenty thousand naira you gave to me
For my final year college tuition
I used it to buy drinks for members
Of the gang, I joined
I am sorry

Victor Ansor

I wish I could pay
Back a hundred-fold

I also joined my friends to
Rob a catholic church in Egerton
Of four bags of cement
They forced me to help them take
The cement since we were
The ones who helped
In the church building project
After high school
We used the money to buy clothes
I have been feeling guilty since
And I promise to pay them back
Next time I am in Calabar
I am sorry mama
I could not bring myself to tell you

Mama, I also want to confide in you
For a long time, I was far away from God
I joined the cult and live a very
Dangerous life
I did not follow His ways
Nor keep His precepts
Sin got a hold of me and
And I struggled with addictions
Captured by powers beyond me
Pushing me to do things I

A Letter To My Late Mom

Would not and pressured
I bent low, sinking so deep into
Sin I struggled

For I long to serve God and do
Right but the opposite is what
I saw myself committed
My heart breaks every time
I pleased the devil with sin
For righteousness pleases God
But sin makes the devil happy

Oh, who can deliver me from
The fangs of wickedness
I cried
That I may serve the Master
He has not dealt with me
According to my sins but shows
Mercy at every turn
Fearful that He may run out of mercy
My heart sinks and breaks
For sin took hold of me
I could not escape

I did not attend church nor
Study the word
I lived very recklessly
But thank God He kept

Me and did not allow me
To die and go to hell
The reason I serve Him now
With all my heart

Life is amazing mama
It is a beautiful thing for
The eye to behold the sun
But as beautiful as life is, it
Is complicated, full of twist and turns
Things appear to be what they
Are not, deceptive as humans
Who may be wearing rags, washing
Toilets in porch buildings, having
The appearance of poverty and
Struggling citizens but beneath
Their basement is
Wealth unimaginable
Even the bank of England may not
Conceal such cash of a lifetime

When you think you know
Life or an individual
Surprisingly, they are cloaked
In deception to your
Outer amazement
When unwrapped
Such is life, mama

A Letter To My Late Mom

Now mama, let me tell
You why you died
What killed you was
Negative confessions
For *life and death are in*
The power of the tongue
So says the scripture
And *a man's belly shall be*
Filled with the fruit of his lips
What we say help
Build our world
You built death with
The fruit of your lips
You kept confessing
Death time and again

I remember when I
Came home one day
You told me how you
Would have died
And you kept saying it
That was wrong mama, very wrong
You do not say what you
Feel or anything negative
Whatever the case, be positive
Trust in God to heal and to protect
Speak health and

Life instead of death
In this, you will live
Longer and live better
If you knew what I know now
You would never have died
For life give to us what we say

Oh, how I miss you, mama,
The beautiful Efik woman
There is no equal
The land misses your very steps
Heaven must be lighted
By your very presence
I hope my daughter
Will look like you
To remind me continually
Of your beauty
With a heart of gold, you
Ruled your house
We miss you, mama, your
Children miss you dearly

Oh, mama where are you
I called out but you do not
Answer, I weep but none to comfort
Your demise is as fresh as when you
Left, that morning you appeared
To me to call my brother

A Letter To My Late Mom

Early in the morning, you never
Did that, I called and heard voices
My siblings arguing about calling
Me, there I heard you passed
I broke down and wept and
Refused to be comforted

I wept on the street and in the parks
On the bus, to Calabar, I wept
And refused comfort
Could not believe you passed
I tried to wake up but each
Seconds proved real
My spirit breaks and never mended
I miss you, mama,
Will always do

Mama, at your funeral
People said good things about you
The way it is expected
Except yours was true
Nobody lied about
Your life here on earth
As they do with other people
Who though may not have lived
Right, received a good report
Which is but a lie
It is better to live well here in life

So, the clergy won't lie at the funeral
Yours was true I bet my life on it

Mama, what people thought I would
Never become I have and still climbing
The time lost because of
Not listening to you
I have redeemed
This is pure grace from God
Because not everyone
Has such an opportunity

I am where no one in the
Family ever stepped
I have what others see as far fetched
Achieving what many see as impossible
I am blessed
I am made

There is no self-made man, mama
Everyman is made by God
And since God does
Not come in person
He sends men
For when God wants to bless a man
He sends a man

A Letter To My Late Mom

One cannot claim to be self-made
When they have input
From different sources
Those who work for us, help made us
Our spouse, friends, or family
Are part of our making
It is wrong to say one is self-made

Mama, the earth is infected
With a dangerous virus
Called coronavirus
It happened while
Trying to send this letter
The world is on a lockdown
Nations and cities deserted
The like no one ever imagined

In New York, the city that never sleeps
Is sleeping for the first time
Busy alleys and driveways now
Inhabited by pigeons and rodents

It is a purging moment for the world
And a wakeup call for God's children
That their redemption is near
It is a furnace that will bring
Us out purified like gold

Victor Ansor

It surprises me mama
That no pastor is preaching about
The end times
Despite the Bible warning that
Pestilence will happen before the end
Instead, they see the pandemic
As an assault from hell
Aim at Christians to perish
So, they curse, bind, and lose
While the devil laughs and party
At their ignorance of times and seasons

Men of God who supposed
To preach the gospel
To calm the heart of followers
And let them know the end
Is near, abandon such
To concoct rubbish on social
Media for the gullible masses
To consume and sometimes
Display gross ignorance of issues
When they have the bible
As a perfect guide

Churches are empty and stores closed
No one in the offices and many
Are in great despair
Jobs are lost and bills pilling

A Letter To My Late Mom

Who would have believed that
A time will come when Easter and
Sunday services will not hold
And everyone asked to stay home
When what we thought matter
Holds no water and everything
Becomes meaningless except life

Mama, do you know what a hashtag is?
I bet you don't
The world is trending on a hashtag now
COVID-19, self-isolation, social distancing
Quarantine and flatten the curve
New words that dominate
Our everyday lives until it ends
I mean beautiful words that
Has come to redefine the way
We live mama
Life will never be the same after this
Pray for the world mama
It is awfully bad

People wear a mask as in the movies
Husband and wife set apart
Each becoming suspicious who
Has the virus
Families on the verge

Victor Ansor

Of breaking apart
Neighbors no longer
Trust one another
The world has changed
Not the way we knew it

Mama, New Yorkers proved
Themselves to be New Yorkers indeed
They surely don't run
Away from trouble
But run towards it
Like the case of nine eleven
They prove themselves again
Many have lost their lives on the
Frontline of the war
Against coronavirus
Yet many still launch
Towards it fearless
It is the New York spirit, mama
Everyone finds a way to help
In profession and gifts
They fight to see victory at the end
I am proud to live here mama

God can allow the pandemic but
He is not responsible
We blame Him always instead
Of looking at the right source

A Letter To My Late Mom

The devil
For his mandate is to
Steal, kill and destroy
But the everlasting Father gives
Life in abundance
The world should know

The reason God permits outbreaks
Is to fulfill his end-time agenda
To see if men will repent and
Seek after Him
So, He can heal and bless them

The world is coming to an end
And few are aware
For if all knew then there
Will be no panic
For it was prophesied and kept
In the bible
The very reason why we should open it

I will tell you more after your reply
Remain ever bath in heavenly light
Your loving son, Papa

Other Poems Written by the Author

Fatherless

I have a father
Or at least I do
Else how did I come to be
I never knew my father
He was never there
From the moment I screamed
I never saw him
Not a glimpse of his feature
Absent as it seems

Never know what it feels like
To have a father
Grew up alone, alone indeed
Naked and shameless
I roam the earth
No one to show me the way

I tied my shoes
Took my bath
Combed my hair
Walked naked till I was ten
He was never there

Victor Ansor

None to pat my shoulder
When I make a mark

Don't know what it feels
Like to have a father
No influence, no advice
No rebuke when I go wrong
Lived by trial and error
Made mistakes, paid the price
Oh, what a world of the fatherless

Had my first kiss
When I was eighteen
None told me the dread
Of teenage woes
Nor diseases that swim
The world of sex
I dived headlong
Sampling as I go
Addicted to pleasure
I made my bed with girls

Traveled the long road alone
No one gives a hand
No advice, from a father I need
He was never there
Loads of errors, void of correction

A Letter To My Late Mom

A fatherless world
A boy should avoid
If he must be a man
Absentee father
The ruin of our time

Pen of A Ready Writer

I have written a timeless piece
My heart's been full of wisdom
Or inspiration at it best
A lot has come out of me
Yet still consume with more to give
Can never exhaust His gifts
Still have more to give

Oh, were I with a thousand hand
To write when He speaks
In my limitation
Still fill with gifts
Can never exhaust His gifts

He speaks every moment
As the bird sings
As the water cries
With drops and spill
The wind spells a thing
All I do is write
Can never exhaust His gifts

A Letter To My Late Mom

Let me die the death of the righteous
Let my end be glorious
But all that is in me
For a thousand generation
Can never exhaust His gifts in me

Give me the words
When I lack of it
Tell me in tongues
When my mind cannot understand
I am a pen of a ready writer
Can never exhaust His gifts

My Lady

She is an epitome of refinement
The very essence of love
With perfect ambiance
And cruel seductive contours
Carried away
With such refurbish atrocious audacity
Went on bended knees
And many supplications offered
With reckless abandonment
Of immediate cosmic existence
The flow of endless appeal
Of nature drop falling
Of aroused, intense, rhythmic persistence
Needless dumbfounded and much perplex
I held my peace

Wild and Free

When I was young
I did the things I wanted
But now that am old
Someone holds my hands
Taking me where I don't want to go

Hold my hands
Never let go
Take me where I should be
Not where I want to go

I was young and free
Like wild orchid
I grew without bounds
With so much liberty and pride
Doing the things, I wanted

For life is a gift
Beautiful as it is
With much to desire
An unending wave of much to achieve

katko vs Briney

A thief a thief
The owner screams
From a distance
An old farmhouse stood

Where is my gun
My old spring gun
My protector my defense
An Intruder beware
Or lose a leg

Katko the thief
Smooth as a disc
Trespassing and ignoring
The warning of sign

Blown in pieces
His leg demise
The court is waiting
The case will be judged

A Letter To My Late Mom

Oh, my house
My lovely farmhouse
Now is lost
With no money for the judge
I've lost everything
to Katko the thief

The Sinner

A hypocrite among the brethren
A double life I've come to live
The Bonds of Hades take hold
A grip so strong
I can't seem to detach
Caught in a web of sin
Swallowed by the very
Pit I walked out from
My soul abhors and detest
Yet I crave unhinge obsession
My life reflects an outcast
Dogs that fall on crumbs
I have become

Oh, wretched man that I am
Who can deliver me and put me up?
To stand in His presence
Without guilt eating me up
Prayer alter is dry
The fire is out
I live only by mercy
On misty eyes

A Letter To My Late Mom

And Secret tears
I wet my bed
Waiting for the redemption
That Seems too far

Father hear me from on high
Stretch out your hand
Hold me strong
Never to fall again
For I have made my bed with sinners
Sending my savior to calvary
Again, and again

www.ingramcontent.com/pod-product-compliance
Lightning Source LLC
Chambersburg PA
CBHW021106080526
44587CB00010B/405